THE DIG-IN WORKBOOK

BY MARTY HAIR

Designer / Illustrator: James Denk
Editor: Renee Murawski
Copy Editor: Will St. John
Photographer: Susan Tusa

Published by
The Detroit Free Press
321 W. Lafayette Blvd.
Detroit, Mich. 48226

Manufactured in the United States of America

ISBN 0-937247-64-2

INDEX

Introduction 5
January 7-16
February 17-26
March 27-36
April 37-46
May 47-56
June 57-66
July 67-76
August 77-86
September 87-96
October 97-106
November 107-116
December 117-126
How to build a compost pile 127
A gardener's glossary 128-129
Gardens to visit 130-133
Planning grids 134-137
Notes 138-141
Phone numbers 142
Garden receipts 143
USDA Plant Hardiness Zone Map 144

Each year in the garden has a distinctive rhythm, and this book provides a place to track it.

Keep notes of weather, pests and remedies, treatments and fertilizers. Map new flower beds. Include photos, sales receipts and the dates plants bloom or bear fruit, as well as what to move and what to try another season.

Within the pages for each week, you will find suggested garden chores as well as space for your own observations, a personal reference for future years.

Planting and pruning, staking up and cutting back — it's a life-and-death drama out there. Do what must be done, but don't bog down in duties. Leave plenty of time to enjoy your garden.

Because, as they say, the best thing about gardening is that there's always next year.

My thanks go to Dr. J. Lee Taylor, horticulture professor emeritus at Michigan State University, who graciously reviewed this manuscript and made valuable suggestions. Many tips in this book are based on information from MSU Extension publications.

This book is dedicated to my family and to the late Betty Frankel, the Detroit Free Press garden writer for nearly a quarter century. Her enthusiasm and knowledge continue to inspire thousands of us who garden in Michigan.

"There is no mystery about gardening, just the wondrous fact that seed time and harvest occur each year, generation after generation, wherever the soil is tilled. If gardeners do their part they can confidently expect the miracle to continue as it has through all time."

— James Underwood Crockett,

"Crockett's Victory Garden"

Week 1

Resolve to complete a specific garden task in the next two months, before the action picks up outside:

Build a bench or trellis. Construct a cold frame. Read up on new techniques or specific plants to try this year.

■ Start the new year with fresh green, courtesy of the kitchen: Put carrot tops in a shallow dish of water. Suspend an avocado seed with toothpicks over a glass of water. Twist the prickly top off a pineapple, remove a half-inch or so of the lower leaves and let the top dry for a day before planting in soil.

■ Your garden would be glad to get an aging Christmas tree, if you have one: Use its branches to mulch perennials. Prop up the tree and hang suet and birdseed balls on it until spring. Or chip it in a shredder, either for your yard or at a municipal collection station.

NOTES

Week 2

Houseplants do more than cheer the spirit. They actually remove chemical pollutants from the air. However, they need extra care in the winter to compensate for weak light and overheating.

Set the pots atop a tray of pebbles and add water to the tray to boost humidity around the plants. Make sure to leave a space between the waterline and the bottom of the pots.

This also improves drainage; extra water drips out of the drainage hole into the pebble layer.

Do not use softened water on houseplants. It may cause root damage and leaf burn.

N O T E S

Week 3

For evergreens, late winter can be deadly. Foliage that is warmed by the sun during the day can freeze at night. In addition, moisture lost can't be replaced through the roots because the ground may be frozen.

In severe cases, the plant may suffer winter burn and actually look scorched come April or May. Preventing that is the purpose of putting burlap screens around evergreens. (Don't use plastic as a screen — it holds too much heat.)

To reduce the chance of sun scald and frost cracks, wrap trunks of young trees with foil, use a commercial tree-wrap product or give the bark a coat of white latex paint.

■ Gently sweep powdery snow from evergreens.

If the branches are coated with ice, leave them alone or they may break off.

■ Broadleaf evergreens in particular benefit from a coating of anti-desiccant spray, because they can lose so much water through their leaves. Such sprays should be applied when the temperature is above 40.

February thaw, anyone?

NOTES

Week 4

Grow something. Start basil or lettuce from seeds sown under fluorescent lights that remain on 16 hours a day (an inexpensive lamp timer can make this easy). Grow bean or other sprouts in a jar for a fast and tasty salad harvest.

■ If you had the foresight last fall to prepare tulip, crocus or daffodil bulbs for forcing, congratulations! Now's the time to start bringing the bulbs out of cold storage — a pot or two a week, if you have that many. Set the pots in a cool, dim spot for a few days, then bring them into the warmer living areas.

■ Winter is a good time to photograph your yard for future reference. Tour a park, botanical garden or arboretum to see landscape plants with attractive bark, stem color or fruits for this time of year.

■ Put sand or fireplace ashes instead of salt on icy walks; this will prevent salt damage to plants and lawns.

"Nature writes, gardeners edit."

— Roger Swain,

"Groundwork, a Gardener's Ecology"

Week 1

Starting seeds indoors gives you a greater variety of plants, may save money compared to buying transplants and can give you a jump on the growing season.

Most importantly, it gives anxious gardeners something to do while awaiting spring.

Use vermiculite or a sterile soilless mix for germinating seeds. This reduces the chance of damping off, a fungal disease that causes newly sprouted seedlings to keel over and die.

Wet the medium before sowing seed. Use only containers with drainage holes.

Mist after planting. Keep containers covered with clear plastic (a plastic bag works well) until seeds germinate.

■ Keep growing seedlings in a south-facing window or under fluorescent lights — one cool white bulb and one warm white bulb.

■ When seedlings have two sets of leaves, transplant them to roomier containers if they're not already in a cell pack or pot. Fill the new container with sterile potting soil amended with peat, vermiculite or perlite. Transfer the transplants by holding the leaves, not the stems. Feed with a water-soluble fertilizer at half the recommended strength.

N O T E S

Week 2

Help Valentine's Day bouquets last longer by removing leaves that will be below water level.

To make sure the flowers can take up enough water, remove about an inch of stem, cutting on a slant.

Add a floral preservative to the water, or mix your own with equal parts water and lemon-lime soft drink, plus a few drops of chlorine bleach.

■ Over the next six weeks, a few well-selected branches brought indoors will bloom and contribute a welcome suggestion of spring. Forsythia is the obvious choice, but many woody plants are excellent for forcing into flower indoors.

On a day the temperature rises above freezing, cut branches of redbud, Japanese quince, fruit trees, or red and silver maples. Bring the branches inside and put them in a bucket of warm water in a dim room with a temperature of about 60 degrees until the flower buds start to open.

NOTES

Week 3

Seeds from last year may still be viable if they have been stored in a cool, dry place. Test-germinate a dozen between damp paper towels inside a plastic bag.

If half the seeds sprout, expect roughly 50 percent germination from the remainder.

■ Do a houseplant bed check. Are roots growing out the bottom of the pot, or encircling the soil when you gently lift up the plant? Late winter is a good time for repotting. Choose a new container with a drainage hole and a diameter an inch or two larger than the old pot.

■ As days grow brighter, increase water for houseplants. Moisten the soil before applying fertilizer.

NOTES

Week 4

Prepare for spring. Treat clay pots to a soak and scrub. Loosen accumulated salts with a mixture of 10 parts water to one part household bleach.

■ Sharpen your tools. If the mower needs professional attention, make arrangements now.

■ Potted hardy bulbs purchased in bloom for indoor use may be saved and planted outdoors later. When flowers fade, remove the bloom and stem from tulips, crocuses, hyacinths and daffodils — but leave the leaves to continue growing. Move the pots to a sunny indoor spot and give them regular water and fertilizer. When foliage dries, store the bulbs in a cool, dry place. Save them for use in the fall.

■ If you stored geraniums in paper bags last fall, retrieve them, pot them in a soil mix, cut them back to 3-5 inches and fertilize. The plants will likely start growing again and may even flower eventually.

NOTES

"For, lo, the winter is past,

the rain is over and gone;

the flowers appear on the earth;

the time of the singing of birds is

come, and the voice of the turtle is

heard in our land."

— The Song of Solomon

Week 1

Finish ordering seeds and plants for this spring.

On Pages 134-137, draw up a plan of new landscape ideas to inspire you later this season.

■ Save rinsed eggshells to crush and sprinkle around hostas this summer to foil slugs.

■ Record when the first snowdrops, squills and winter aconites bloom and where, then make a note for the first week in September to order early bulbs.

■ Prune grapevines.

Week 2

Late winter and early spring are pruning season for many deciduous shrubs and trees. Before new leaves appear, the plant's natural shape is readily apparent, and pruning now helps stimulate healthy new growth.

But for spring-flowering shrubs such as lilac, forsythia, mock orange, crabs or weigela, wait to prune until just after the plants bloom; otherwise, you'll be sacrificing this year's flowers. Prune evergreens in May after their first spurt of new growth.

As you prune, remove dead or damaged branches, as well as suckers and watersprouts, those pencil-like whips that spurt up from the base or straight up from the branches.

Next, trim off branches that rub against each other. Make the cut just above the branch collar, the swollen ring where the branch meets the trunk. The plant will heal itself. Dressing or otherwise covering the wound is no longer recommended.

Pruning should follow the plant's natural shape, as well as open it to sunlight and air circulation.

When shaping a deciduous hedge, keep the top slightly narrower than the bottom to allow more light to reach inside.

Week 3

The soil is ready to work for cool crops when it thaws and passes the squeeze test: Take a handful of soil, squeeze it and release. If it remains in a clump, it's too wet to work. The soil will compact and seeds may rot. Wait until the soil is crumbly, then plant lettuce, peas, spinach, broccoli, beets, radishes, onions, parsnips, Swiss chard and kale. Sandy soil and raised beds will be ready the earliest.

■ Remove mulch gently from around early spring bulbs, but keep it handy in case the weather turns cold suddenly. Remove old leaves in stages. Compost the leaves or save them to dig into garden beds later this spring.

■ Clean up winter debris, such as branches and twigs.

■ Use a horticultural oil spray to suffocate scale, mites and aphids that have plagued euonymous, lilac or other plants.

Dormant oils may be applied before the buds swell and when the temperature is above 40 and will stay above freezing for at least 24 hours. Check the label for directions and to make sure it is safe to use on your plant. Summer oils are similar but may be applied during the growing season.

N O T E S

Week 4

Fertilize trees and shrubs before mid-April, or when leaves emerge. Use a food high in nitrogen (the first of the three numbers listed on fertilizers) for trees and evergreens. For flowering ornamentals, use a balanced formula such as 12-12-12.

■ Check plants for the egg masses of gypsy moths before the eggs hatch in May. The egg masses are generally in hidden spots, such as under branches or loose bark. The egg masses are light tan.

Egg masses may be scraped off the plant and destroyed by burning or burying 6-8 inches deep.

■ Cut back asparagus, ornamental grasses, sedum and other perennials that were spared a shearing last fall.

NOTES

"I notice that it is only when my mother is working in her flowers that she is radiant, almost to the point of being invisible — except as Creator: hand and eye. She is involved in the work her soul must have."

— Alice Walker,

"In Search of Our Mothers' Gardens"

Week 1

Rake the lawn lightly to lift matted grass and remove dead material. Wait until at least mid-May to fertilize healthy, established lawns, especially those fed late last fall.

■ Lawn aeration makes holes in compacted or heavy clay soil. That allows water, air and nutrients to reach the grass roots, making space for roots to grow.

Aeration may be done anytime. If the lawn is dry, water the night before you aerate, to soften it.

■ Tree wraps applied during a newly planted tree's first or second winter should be taken off in the spring.

If left intact, they may promote girdling or mask signs of insect or disease problems.

■ Mulch can delay soil warming by two weeks or more. Wait to apply mulch until after the soil temperature warms.

■ Start planting perennials.

Week 2

Dig the planting hole for trees and shrubs 50 percent wider and about the same depth as the root ball. If the plant is in a container, slit and remove it before planting. If the plant is balled and burlapped, cut the twine and pull down the burlap from the sides. Remove plastic-coated coverings completely.

■ Spring rains, or you, should soak newly planted trees and shrubs every 7 to 10 days.

■ Set your lawn mower's blade height to 2½ to 3 inches. Mow often enough so you cut no more than one-third of the grass height at one time. Tall grass shades the soil, discouraging weeds and slowing moisture loss. Leave clippings to decompose on the grass, providing a nutrient boost.

■ Apply pre-emergent crabgrass controls before forsythia finishes blooming.

Week 3

Fertilize most perennials before planting and as growth begins in the spring. After that, they may not require feeding every single year. Exceptions are astilbes, chrysanthemums, delphiniums, lupines and garden phlox. These do best with annual fertilization.

■ If pachysandra looks yellow or tired, cutting or even mowing off old foliage will encourage handsome new growth.

■ Spot-seed bare patches in the lawn.

Turn over the soil at least 3 to 4 inches deep. Remove weeds. In heavy clay, work in topsoil or compost. Rake the surface, then sow seed and water lightly daily to keep the soil moistened for the first several weeks. Mow when the new grass reaches about 2½ to 3 inches.

NOTES

Week 4

Winter protection should be removed from roses by now. Finish pruning hybrid teas, grandifloras and floribundas. Cut them back to 12 inches overall, then remove dead wood. Prune until there is white or white-green in the cane's center, then again to just above an outward-facing bud.

Choose the spot for your roses carefully: They want 6-8 hours of sun a day, as much as possible in the morning.

Plant bare root roses. (Container-grown roses and other perennials, trees and shrubs may be planted throughout the season but need extra water during hot weather.) Mix in bone meal or superphosphate with the soil and compost during planting. Make a mound in the center of the planting hole and place the rose on top, then spread the roots and cover with soil.

■ Replant cool weather vegetables — carrots, lettuces, peas, radishes, spinach, Swiss chard — that did not come up from your first planting.

NOTES

"Gardening imparts an organic perspective on the passage of time. It bestows on its practitioners a genuine sense of admiration for the plants, the soil, the sun, the water."

— Jim Nollman,

"Why We Garden"

Week 1

Plant clematises in a well-drained spot with good sun. This vine may be paired with a rose or small tree. The clematis can climb on the other plant instead of a fence or trellis. Clematises require plenty of water throughout the growing season. Keep the roots cool with mulch.

■ Apply mulch when the weather and soil have warmed up. Wood chips, newspaper, straw and cocoa hulls are a few of the possibilities. To avoid trapping moisture, keep mulch 2 to 3 inches away from the plant's crown.

Decomposing wood chips and sawdust can deplete nitrogen in the soil; look for a slow-release source to compensate, either organic or inorganic. Don't use plain peat as a mulch on top of the soil. It makes a barrier that keeps water from plant roots.

■ Compost improves both heavy clay and sandy soils. If you haven't already, set aside room in the garden now to start a compost pile.

See instructions on Page 127.

NOTES

Week 2

Before mid-month, remove deadwood from climbers, shrub roses and ramblers. Cut back evergreens to about half the length of new green growth.

■ Harden off young seedlings by getting them used to the outdoors for about 10 days before planting time. Put them outside, starting in a shady place and gradually increasing the amount of light to which they are exposed. Bring them in at night if unseasonably cold weather threatens.

■ Feed spring bulbs once more and snip off old flowers but leave foliage to ripen. Feed roses after growth has begun in the spring and the danger of frost is past, and again about 4-6 weeks later.

■ Plant hardy annuals and more perennials. Finish planting bare root trees and shrubs this month.

■ Put up 18-inch-high rabbit fence to protect lettuce, peas, carrots and other crops.

■ Plant beans. There's only a small chance of injury from frost. Start planting sweet corn and continue through the month.

NOTES

Week 3

Dig and divide garden chrysanthemums for best flower production. Replant 18 inches apart.

After danger of frost has passed, plant petunias, geraniums, portulaca, begonias, impatiens, caladiums, coleus. Start planting dahlias, glads and cannas, and continue each week through June for staggered bloom. Work in fertilizer around tender bulbs before planting.

■ Established lawns may be fed now through early June.

■ Pinch back phlox to about five stems to improve bloom and air circulation, the bane of powdery mildew.

■ Once the weather is reliably warm, it is safe to move houseplants outside if it's easier for you to care for them there during the summer. Keep them in filtered shade, not full sun. Monitor their water needs and check often for insects.

■ Start herbs in regular soil with good sun and drainage. Plant basil, chives, dill, parsley, rosemary and others according to your cooking style. Keep mint growing in a sunken or raised container; planted directly in the garden it will run far and wide.

Week 4

Prune spring-flowering shrubs, such as forsythia and lilac, after they finish blooming.

■ Plant bright-colored annuals where you want to attract attention, such as at a door or on patio steps.

■ Plant tomatoes, cucumbers, squash, pumpkins, melons, peppers and eggplant when all danger of frost is past.

■ When planting in containers, make sure each pot has a drainage hole. Containers should be at least 8 inches deep. The smaller the container, the faster it will dry out.

To make pots look full, put container plants closer together than you would in a garden. As flowers on ornamental plants fade, pick off old blooms. Mulch will help hold the moisture. Even so, containers may require watering every day.

N O T E S

"Summer afternoon — summer afternoon; to me those have always been the two most beautiful words in the English language."

— Henry James

Week 1

If you plan to add sweet violets or other edible flowers to a salad or dessert, make sure the plant has not been sprayed with chemicals. Wash flowers well to remove dirt and gently shake dry.

■ When starting nasturtiums from seed, soak them overnight before planting.

■ Feed acid-loving plants — rhododendrons, azaleas, dogwood, hollies — with a fertilizer formulated especially for these plants.

■ Put up a rabbit fence around beans, or plant them near lettuce and other crops that are already fenced.

■ Sprinkle clean, crushed egg shells around hostas to deter slugs. Or use diatomaceous earth or gravel, commercial slug bait or saucers of beer.

NOTES

Week 2

To encourage bushier plants, pinch back the growing tips of hardy chrysanthemums when they are 6 inches tall. Repeat about the second week of July, then let the plant develop.

■ Cabbage maggots may be a problem for crops like cabbage, broccoli, kale, cauliflower and turnips. If plants already are wilted, it's too late. When you make a second planting for fall harvest, make a snug-fitting collar of rubber, Naugahyde or other material around the stem to prevent cabbage maggot larvae from reaching the roots.

■ Cutworms are especially fond of young seedlings. Make a collar for growing cabbage, broccoli, cauliflower, pepper and tomato plants from paper milk cartons, paper or plastic cups or tin cans with the tops and bottoms removed.

Some gardeners trick the night-feeding cutworms with a fatal attraction — a mix of bran and molasses in a line leading away from the vegetables. The cutworms eat the mixture and die or get stuck.

■ Gently pull ripe peas from plants so they will continue producing. When the harvest is finished, compost the pea vines, which are rich in nitrogen.

■ Be vigilant with weeds, which are much easier to pull when they are small and the soil is moist.

Week 3

Make a circle of ground cover, mulch or annuals around trees to keep lawn mowers away from the trunks.

■ Stake tall plants or enclose them in wire tomato cages.

■ Discourage powdery mildew by keeping water off foliage. Use a soaker hose and water in the morning or early afternoon, not evening.

■ After Oriental poppies fade, the foliage will shrink and die. Plant annuals or such perennials as baby's breath *(Gypsophila paniculata)* to fill in.

■ Keep the vegetable garden occupied.

As early crops are harvested, fill in with another crop of beans, corn, cucumbers, lettuce, beets, carrots, zucchini or other summer squash.

N O T E S

Week 4

When June-bearing strawberries finish producing, fertilize the plants and cultivate surrounding soil to entice runners to spread. A new plant should form about every 12 inches.

■ Give tomatoes regular water to reduce the chance of blossom-end rot. Mulching them helps retain moisture.

While you're at it, water the compost pile to speed decomposition.

■ Some stores will put seeds away soon. Buy a few packets of perennials to plant next month.

■ Plant more annual poppies and marigolds for a late-season color blast.

N O T E S

"Toward the end of the first decade of gardening you are poised between the garden of your fantasies and your slowly accumulating knowledge of what you may actually achieve someday. This is very similar to the stage of life in which you realize that you will never be as rich, as powerful, as clever, as seductive, as young as the images with which the world surrounds you."

— Patricia Thorpe,

"Growing Pains: Time and Change in the Garden"

Week 1

If you're going on a trip, your garden will be home alone. To help it survive on autopilot:

Water vegetables, flower beds and the lawn generously.

Trim the lawn a bit shorter than usual.

Mulch beds and vegetables to hold moisture.

Deadhead fading flowers and cut petunias way back to promote later flowering.

Move containers into the shade and apply mulch. Set up fiber wick systems, available at many garden centers, to provide moisture, or ask a neighbor to water the pots.

For a continuous source of moisture:

Take a clean, empty plastic milk jug and fill with water. Then punch a small hole in the bottom of the jug. Set the jug in the vegetable garden, where it will slowly release the water for a couple of days.

NOTES

Week 2

The vegetable garden can use a high-nitrogen booster fertilizer as mid-season approaches.

■ Keep up an even supply of moisture for the vegetables. Fertilize tomatoes after small ones have formed to boost output.

■ White flowers in the garden perform as night lights. They will brighten corners and the back porch or patio where you can appreciate them in the evening.

■ Vigilance pays off with roses. Spray regularly to prevent fungus and insect damage. Feed roses with fertilizer low in nitrogen and high in phosphorous. Make this the last feeding of the year so new growth will have time to harden before cold weather arrives.

■ If evergreens have a faded, dusty look, check for spider mites. Shake a branch over a piece of white paper. Tiny, moving dark spots are mites. Wash the shrubs, especially the undersurface, with the hose, or use insecticidal soap.

■ Set the lawn mower to 3 inches. Don't fertilize the lawn until September.

N O T E S

Week 3

What's eating the garden? While vegetables and grass keep growing, so does the number of nibbling critters.

■ Aphids are sap-sucking bugs that love roses. Remove them using a strong spray of water early in the day, twice a week for several weeks.

Earwigs may attack flowers and leaves. They love dark, damp places. Remove mulch right around plants and the foundation.

■ Water drought-stressed grass.

■ Plant peas around July 15 for harvest in September.

■ Thickly planted kale and collards can be thinned to 8 inches apart. Eat the thinnings.

Week 4

Dig and divide bearded irises now through mid-August. Plants that are 4 or 5 years old will have grown into dense clumps, and flower production will be declining. Divide Japanese and Siberian irises in August.

Here's the drill for any type of iris:

Lift out the clump, hose it down and cut the fleshy rhizomes into divisions.

Discard spongy pieces.

Dust rhizomes with powdered sulfur and let them dry for a day.

Replant where there is good drainage and work in compost. Barely cover the rhizomes with new soil, then water in.

Trim back foliage to a few inches in late fall; destroy the cut leaves, which may contain borer eggs.

Mulch newly divided irises the first winter.

"Weeds live an extremely long time in the waiting seed stage. Five years is common, a dozen years is not unheard of, and there are even reports of a seed which has been caught in Arctic gravel and revived, to grow successfully, after a dormancy stretching from 6,000 B.C."

— David Bodanis,

"The Secret Garden"

Week 1

Shades of blue can cool down the hottest flower beds in the stickiest weather. For mid- to late-summer perennial blue color, make a note to yourself to consider adding bellflower *(Campanula* sp.), balloon flower *(Platycodon grandiflorus),* globe thistle *(Echinops ritro),* lavender *(Lavandula angustifolia),* Russian sage *(Perovskia atriplicifolia)* or other sages *(Salvia* sp.). Some hostas have bluish flowers.

■ Harvest herbs for preserving in late morning on a sunny day. Use only healthy, undamaged leaves. Shake off soil. Wipe leaves clean or wash gently. Tie stems with a rubber band, then hang the bunch in a warm, dry place. Herb leaves may also be put out to dry on a piece of screen. Store dried herbs in an airtight jar away from light.

Basil, cilantro and dill are good candidates for freezing. Clean, dry and wrap them tightly, like a log, in plastic. To use, unwrap, snip off the amount needed and replace the rest in the freezer.

■ Keep watering and weeding around tomatoes and the rest of the vegetable garden.

NOTES

Week 2

Plant another round of cool-weather vegetables, including leaf lettuce, kale, spinach, mustard greens and radishes.

■ If yellow jackets are a problem, figure out where they live. The papery wasp nest may be underground or above ground. Unless the nest is next to the house or some other spot where it can't be avoided, give it a wide berth and just leave it alone. If you must, spray the nest with an insecticide containing carbaryl. Apply at dusk, then leave the area pronto.

Don't use carbaryl inside or on the house structure.

■ Perk up tired annuals with a water-soluble fertilizer high in phosphorus, the middle of the three numbers on fertilizer packages.

■ White pine weevil larvae can stunt growth and cause the tips of white, Scotch, Austrian pines, some firs and blue spruce to droop. Watch for signs of curving, also called "shepherd's crook." Prune out damaged tips but wait to spray until next April.

■ Transplant or move Oriental poppies, which are now dormant. Be careful, because they have long, brittle roots.

NOTES

Week 3

Now through mid-September is the best time to start grass from seed. Days are warm, nights are cooling off and rain is usually plentiful. To grow new seed in an existing lawn, see instructions on Page 42.

■ Check established lawns for white grubs. Japanese beetle larvae feed on grass roots, leaving brown areas that lift easily. Damage is worst now through next month. Grubs are usually found curved like the letter "C." The best defense is maintaining a healthy lawn through proper mowing, feeding and watering. In severe cases, chemical insecticides are available. But these should be used only when the grubs are feeding near ground level, from mid-August to mid-September. Follow label precautions.

Week 4

Red, purple and black raspberry canes that bore fruit earlier this year should be cut off at ground level.

■ If honeysuckle growing tips are tightly clumped, honeysuckle aphid is probably the villain. The only permanent cure is to take out the honeysuckle and plant something else.

■ The season has come to a stall. The light is changing, and so are nighttime temperatures.

Have a party to mark the final week of real summer and to celebrate your hard work in the garden.

NOTES

"The tints of autumn — a mighty flower garden blossoming under the spell of the enchanter, Frost."

— John Greenleaf Whittier

Week 1

In the coming week, round up houseplants that summered outdoors and haul them back inside, giving them a thorough inspection first. Mix a solution of water and a few drops of mild detergent, wash the foliage, then rinse with clear water. Keep plants that were outside isolated from other houseplants for a month or so, in case insects or diseases develop.

■ There are several ways to save geraniums for another season or to enjoy indoors:

1. Take a 3- or 4-inch cutting from stem tips. Strip off all but the top cluster of leaves. Let the cuttings dry for a day, then dip in rooting hormone. Place cuttings in sand or perlite and water every few days. When roots are visible, in about two or three weeks, pot the new plant.

2. Dig up geraniums. Shake off soil. Bring them indoors, storing them in paper bags or hanging the plants upside down in a cool, dark place. Repot in February.

3. Simply bring inside a potted geranium. Prune hard; otherwise geraniums will grow long and spindly in the weak winter light. To encourage winter blooms, place the plant where it will get at least four hours of sun a day.

■ Plan which spring bulbs to plant later this month.

N O T E S

Week 2

Plant peonies this month in a sunny, well-drained location. Sun is essential for good bloom; so is planting depth. Dig a hole at least three times the root size and work in a handful of bone meal. Firm down the bottom of the hole. Place so the "eye," the place on the root where the new bud will sprout, points up and so the tip is no more than 1 1/2 inches below soil level.

■ Plant other perennials, as well as container-grown trees and shrubs.

Wait until October to plant bare root ornamentals.

Water new plants well and mulch early this winter after the ground freezes.

■ Divide daylilies. Dig up the fleshy root mass, slice it apart with a spade or knife and replant the divisions promptly.

■ Fertilize lawns — ideally, just before a rain. Otherwise, water well after the feeding.

NOTES

Week 3

Frost usually comes to southeastern Michigan in October, but it can occasionally occur this month. If an overnight freeze is forecast, protect annuals — especially those growing in low areas, which are particularly vulnerable — and tomatoes, eggplants and peppers. Use sheets, newspapers or plastic. Remove the protective covering the next morning.

■ Gently lift tuberous begonia tubers and caladiums before the first hard freeze. Include some of the surrounding soil and tops. Dry for several weeks. Remove soil and store in sand in a cool, dark place.

■ After their foliage dies, dig gladiolus corms and dahlia tubers. Store in peat or vermiculite in a basement or similar area. Mist the dahlia tubers occasionally; they should not dry out. Divide them next spring.

N O T E S

Week 4

The minor bulbs — which are major when it comes to providing early spring cheer — should be planted this month. These include the squills, crocuses, snowdrops, winter aconites and glories-of-the-snow.

Larger bulbs, such as daffodils, hyacinths and alliums, can be planted in October; tulips can go in the ground into November, so long as the soil can be worked.

When planting bulbs, turn the bed deeper than the bulbs will be planted so the roots will grow easily.

Plant bulbs as soon as possible after their purchase or arrival. They need to be positioned three times as deep as they are high, measured from base to tip. Or plant them according to bulb dealer's instructions. Plant pointed end up. Add a sprinkle of bone meal or bulb fertilizer. Water.

Map where you plant the bulbs on Pages 134-137.

■ Try pairing grape hyacinths with yellow daffodils, crocuses with tulips, pink or other pastel tulips with blue forget-me-nots. Keep this in mind: Subtle color combinations seem artful now, but in early spring the heart and eye are hungry for bold color, for brash reds and yellows. You want to hear a shout that winter is over, not a whisper.

N O T E S

"If we persist, I do not doubt that by

age 96 or so we will all have gardens

we are pleased with, more or less."

— Henry Mitchell

Week 1

Let hydrangea flowers stay right where they are until spring. Like ornamental grasses, the dried hydrangea flower heads provide something to look at in the winter garden. And with these flowering shrubs, pruning now may damage next year's bud, as well as stimulate the plant to send up new growth — just in time to be socked by cold temperatures.

■ Show youngsters how to find seed pods on impatiens, which form in late summer and early fall. Set the largest pods in their palms. Hear the kids squeal as the pods burst open.

■ Move, divide and plant perennials.

■ Keep the rake handy. Promptly remove fallen leaves and add them to their rightful place, the compost pile.

N O T E S

Week 2

Finish planting daffodils, hyacinths and alliums in the next week or two.

■ European white birch is most susceptible to bronze birch borer.

Choose another birch for your fall landscaping plans.

■ Continue planting trees and shrubs, including bare root ornamentals. Dig the planting hole as deep as the root ball and several times wider to accommodate growing roots. Remove container or cut open and fold back burlap. Prune only weak or dead branches.

New trees and shrubs will need at least an inch of water per week throughout the fall.

Week 3

If you plan new perennial beds to plant next spring, prepare the soil now. The area must be well drained. Add compost or other organic matter after turning the soil to 8-12 inches.

■ If the area is covered with grass, rent a sod stripper to remove the turf. Or put down a thick layer of newspaper (regular sections, not color inserts) over the grass; cover with several inches of topsoil. The paper will eventually decompose. Another way to kill the sod is to cover it with black plastic for a few weeks.

■ Set aside a few daffodil, tulip, crocus and hyacinth bulbs for forcing. To be tricked into blooming indoors this winter, the bulbs must spend several weeks in plastic bags in the refrigerator, mulched in a cold frame or in another spot that is no warmer than 40 degrees. Crocuses need six weeks of cold, hyacinths eight, daffodils 10 and tulips 12.

N O T E S

Week 4

Trim iris and peony foliage to several inches and destroy old stalks to avoid spreading diseases and insects. Do not compost these leaves and stems, or any other material that is or might be diseased.

■ After a hard frost, remove annuals and vegetables from the garden. Remove every trace of weeds, including roots. It will make life so much easier next spring.

■ After the plants go dormant, trees, shrubs, vines and ground covers may be fertilized.

■ Rake beds. Turn the soil and work in compost.

■ Call your county office of the MSU Extension to learn how to take a soil test, which is an inexpensive way to measure what nutrients the garden really needs. The soil test measures pH, lime, phosphorus, potassium, calcium and magnesium. Home owners generally get results in two weeks. Test the soil approximately every other year.

"Though an old man,

I am but a young gardener."

— Thomas Jefferson

Week 1

Mow as long as the grass grows. The final cut should be at a height of 1 1/2 to 2 inches.

Then feed the turf one last time. Look for a preparation marked "autumn feed" or one for dormant lawns; some products also kill broadleaf weeds.

Apply before the ground freezes but after mowing season concludes, usually in the first 10 days of November in southeastern Michigan. Grass roots keep growing when the temperature is above 40 degrees.

■ Keep up with raking.

■ Make a final note about annuals — what was successful and what to try. Look around for flowering kale, in full color now for several weeks. Jot down a reminder to plant some next spring.

NOTES

Week 2

Many perennials may be cut back now to just a few inches of stem. Remove clipped foliage for composting. Leave sedum, spiky tall black-eyed Susans and purple coneflower stalks to catch the snow. Trim them back in March, along with ornamental grasses and asparagus.

■ Do not cut growing leaves from perennials that stay green all winter, such as Oriental poppies.

■ Drain outdoor ponds. Clean, then cover with tarps or boards. Store hardy water lilies in their containers at 40 to 55 degrees. Cover the soil with damp organic material so it stays moist.

■ Drain and store hoses. Rinse potted plant containers and stash where they will not freeze.

Week 3

Leave major rose pruning for April. For now, just trim back tall canes that would whip around in the winter wind.

After the ground freezes and roses become dormant, remove and discard fallen rose leaves. Then get the winter protection ready. The idea is to shield the base of the plant.

Cones, cages and other devices may be purchased. Or mound 12 inches of soil from elsewhere in the garden around the plant's base. Or make a chicken wire cage around the rose plant and fill the cage with leaves and soil.

NOTES

Week 4

Winter kill, the combination of repeated daytime sun and nighttime freezes, moisture loss and a late-season frost can leave numerous victims, including privet hedges.

The best defense is to plant hardy trees and shrubs, and to keep the plants' light, soil, drainage, exposure and feeding requirements in mind when locating them on your property.

Landscape plants also profit from having adequate water around their roots before the ground freezes hard.

Broadleaf evergreens such as rhododendrons and azaleas, hollies and euonymous may also be sprayed now with an anti-dessicant, which retards moisture loss over the winter. These should be applied when the temperature is above 40 degrees.

Get the stakes in place for burlap wind screens if they will be used to protect evergreens.

NOTES

"The more one gardens, the more one learns;

and the more one learns, the more one realizes

how little one knows."

— Vita Sackville-West

Week 1

Apply a 3-inch layer of mulch — such as bark, pine needles, hay, shredded leaves — after the ground freezes around perennials and newly planted ornamental landscape plants. The purpose of mulch is not to keep out the cold but rather to keep it in. That lessens damage from repeated freezing and thawing. A thick blanket of snow is one of the best insulators.

■ Once the garden is ready for winter, clean your tools. Wash off any soil, using a wire brush if needed, and wipe dry. Clean wood handles and wipe with linseed oil. Spray metal sections with a lubricant such as WD40.

■ Mount bird feeders and vow to keep them filled until spring.

NOTES

Week 2

Trim holly, juniper, yew, hemlock, spruce and boxwood to use as holiday decorations. Snip young shoots about 4-6 inches long. Greens stay fresh longer if used outdoors. Pine holds its needles well inside, but keep the sticky pitch away from wood finishes and cloth.

Decorate an outdoor tree for the birds. String popcorn, cranberries, cereal, bits of bread.

Indoors, dress up a Norfolk Island pine with ornaments and ribbons.

■ Having a living Christmas tree is a great idea if there is space for it outdoors after the holidays. To survive later, the tree should spend as little time as possible indoors — no more than a week, less if possible. Keep it in a cool spot, on a tray so excess water can drain out, and mist the foliage daily.

To get its outside location ready, dig the hole in advance, while the soil can still be worked. Keep the soil from the planting hole in a sheltered place where it won't freeze before needed.

NOTES

Week 3

When buying a fresh-cut holiday tree, look for green outer foliage. At home, cut off 1⁄4 inch from the base to open the trunk to water.

Check the water reservoir every day. Replenish with plain water. If the tree stem dries out, a seal forms that prevents it from taking in more water. The only recourse then is to take down the tree and recut the stem.

Keep all evergreens and holiday plants away from children and pets, as well as heat, sunlight, candles, fireplaces.

Anchor the Christmas tree well if you have a cat that enjoys climbing trees.

NOTES

Week 4

Poinsettias should have dark, green foliage. Keep them in a room that is 60 to 70 degrees with good natural light and near, but not in, direct sun.

They dislike excessive heat or cold drafts. Move the poinsettias to a cooler room (55 to 60 degrees) at night for longer bloom.

Make sure water can drain from the plants. Remove foil covering or poke holes in it. Put the pots on saucers.

■ If you have a living Christmas tree, plant it outside so it grows at the same depth as it was in the container, then make a burlap cage for it. Place four wooden stakes around the tree and anchor the burlap.

■ Squirrel away mail-order plant catalogs that arrive during the holiday rush.

Anticipate savoring their pages and photos in the new gardening year.

Commercial compost containers are available, but you can make your own for just a few dollars.

Why should you? Because it's great for the garden. Compost recycles nutrients from nature into free food for your plants.

First, find four wood pallets — usually free for the hauling from the supermarket. Tie the pallets together at top and bottom to form the upright sides of a box. Untie and refasten the front as needed for loading or for removing finished compost.

Or you can make a compost holder from a circle of chicken wire tied with fasteners.

Add leaves (shredded ones will decompose faster), grass clippings or other green plant material, and garden soil from elsewhere in the yard. You may also add high-nitrogen fertilizer.

Water the pile so it stays damp, and turn it every week for best results. If you don't turn it, the material still will break down but it will take much longer.

Don't add weeds with seed heads, meat, grease, dairy foods or fish, or any plant matter that is diseased.

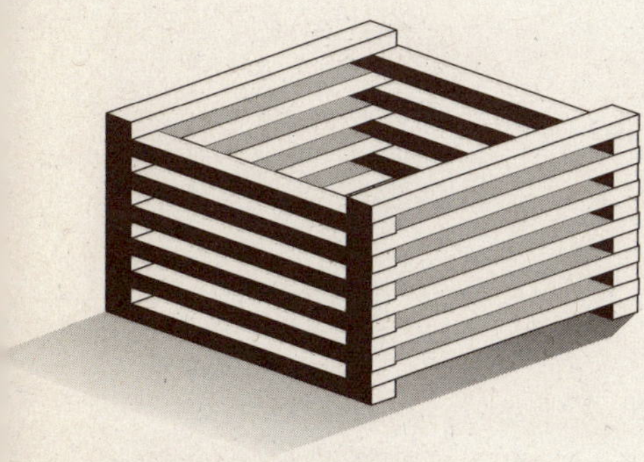

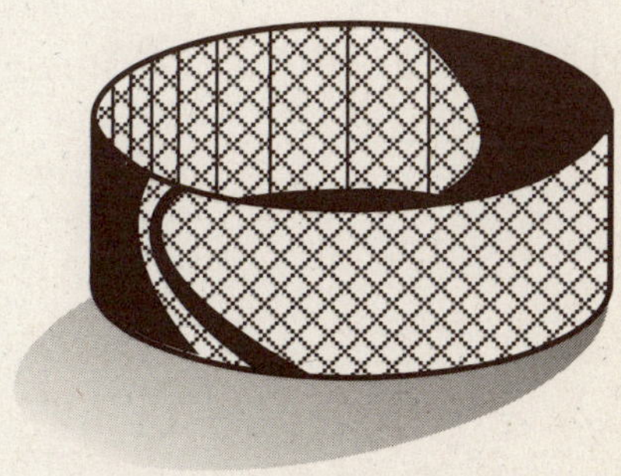

Acid soil: Soil with a pH of less than 7.0.

Alkaline soil: Soil with a pH level greater than 7.0.

Annuals: Plants that begin and complete their life cycle within one year.

Anti-dessicant: Spray used to protect evergreens from moisture loss over winter.

Bare root: A plant without soil around the roots.

Bedding plants: Flowering plants, most often annuals, massed for all-summer color.

Biennials: Plants with a two-year life cycle, producing flowers and seeds in the second year before they die.

Binomial nomenclature: System of plant classification based on Latin genus and species names. For example, the scientific name for Eastern White Pine is *Pinus* (the genus name) *strobus* (the species name). The species may be followed by the variety or cultivar name. *Pinus strobus* 'Nana' is the dwarf Eastern White Pine.

Bracts: Specialized leaves that may be colorful and showy, as on poinsettias.

Bt: *Bacillus thuringiensis,* a bacterium that occurs naturally in soil and on leaves, used in insecticides to kill young caterpillars. Safe for mammals, birds and fish.

Bulb: Swollen underground structure composed mainly of fleshy leaves. Corms, rhizomes and tubers are sometimes included in the general category of bulbs. Example of true bulb: onion.

Cold frame: An enclosed outdoor box with a clear or translucent covering used to grow and force plants while protecting them.

Compost: Decomposed organic material, such as grass clippings and leaves.

Corm: Underground compressed stem that resembles a bulb but has no fleshy scales. A bud or eye may be seen at the top. Tiny new corms, called cormels, form around the parent. Examples: gladiolus, crocus.

Cutting: Part of a plant that has been cut off to start another plant.

Deciduous plants: Those that shed leaves in the fall.

Dormant: Showing little or no growth.

Evergreen: Retains foliage year-round.

Fertilizers: Plant nutrients. Commercial products carry three numbers, signifying the percentages they contain of nitrogen, followed by phosphorus and, as the third number, potassium.

Force: To make a plant flower earlier, usually in response to warmer temperatures.

Germination: Initial growth of the plant from the embryo inside a seed.

Ground cover: Plants grown close together, often low and covering the soil.

Harden off: To expose a plant gradually to a change in conditions, such as colder or windier weather.

Hardiness zone: U.S. Department of Agriculture designations based on average lowest winter temperatures. Plants are described as being hardy to a particular zone. *See map on Page 144.*

Hardy bulbs: Those that can survive outdoors over winter in northern climates. Example: daffodils.

Heavy soil: Dense, often high in clay, slow to drain.

Heaving: The process of a plant's roots being pushed from the ground over winter by the soil's repeated freezing and thawing.

Herbaceous perennial: A

non-woody plant that dies back to the ground each winter; roots remain alive and new growth begins the following season.

Integrated Pest Management (IPM): Strategy of using several tactics — pest identification, monitoring, biological controls, modification of growing conditions and selection of plant varieties — before using chemicals.

Mulch: Natural or synthetic material used to cover the soil between or around plants. Keeps in soil moisture and retards weed growth.

Naturalize: To plant so an area appears as it might in nature.

Nematodes: Tiny worms that may be garden pests or, occasionally, beneficials.

Neutral soil: Having a pH of approximately 7.0.

Node: Place where leaves are located on a stem.

Organic fertilizer: Made all or mostly of decomposed or fresh natural materials, such as manure or compost.

Perennials: Plants whose roots continue to produce new growth for several years, such as asparagus and peony.

Perlite: A natural volcanic material that is crushed and heated, then expands into spongy kernels or pellets. Used as a sterile additive to make a soil mix lighter.

pH: Measure of acidity or alkalinity.

Pinch back: To remove growing tips.

Rhizomes: Thick underground stems, sometimes called rootstock, rhizomes grow horizontally and are usually near the surface, as in bearded iris. New roots grow from the bottom and new shoots from the upper surface.

Rooting hormone: Chemical used on cuttings to promote root growth.

Shoot: New growth, as from a root, bulb, tuber, rhizome or seed.

Side-dressing: Fertilizing around established plants or between rows.

Soilless mix: Growing media with a combination of non-soil materials, such as peat, ground bark, sand, vermiculite and perlite.

Soil test: Measurement of nutrients, deficiencies, pollutants.

Sphagnum moss: Acidic, water-retentive material made from partly decomposed mosses.

Stolon: Fleshy or somewhat woody stem, usually at the surface, that gives rise to new roots at a node. Example: strawberry runners, spider plant.

Tender bulbs: Those which, in northern climates, would not survive the winter outdoors, although many may be placed outside in the warmer months. Example: amaryllis.

Thatch: Undecomposed grass roots, stems, woody parts on soil surface.

Transplant solution: Diluted liquid fertilizer given to new plants to help them get established.

Tuber: Enlarged and fleshy, usually underground, stems with growth buds or eyes, the starting point for new shoots and roots. Example: caladium, potato.

Tuberous roots: Tuber-like underground roots that grow in a clump and may be separated for new plants. Example: dahlia.

Vermicomposting: Use of worms to speed decomposition of organic material.

Vermiculite: Mica mineral that is heated and separates into cell-like chunks. Used as a sterile soil additive; retains water.

Winter burn: Scorching of evergreens during winter through exposure to repeated warming and freezing, as well as wind. Plant loses water from leaves but cannot replenish it because soil is frozen.

Woody plants: Trees, shrubs and vines with woody trunks and stems that persist and grow through all seasons.

This list includes many Michigan and nearby garden destinations. Call before departing to check special exhibits, restrictions or hours.

Albion

WHITEHOUSE NATURE CENTER,
adjacent to the Albion College campus; 1-517-629-2030 during nature center hours. The 135-acre area includes trails as well as a butterfly and a wildflower garden. Grounds are open dawn to dusk daily. Free. Nature center building, open 9:30-4:30 weekdays and 10:30-4:30 weekends except major holidays and some college holidays, is accessible to wheelchair users.

Ann Arbor

MATTHAEI BOTANICAL GARDENS,
1800 N. Dixboro Road; 1-313-998-7060 anytime. Part of the University of Michigan, the 250-acre garden includes bogs, upland forest and meadow, a herb knot garden, roses, wildflowers, nature trails and a conservatory. Grounds are open 8 a.m.-sunset daily, the conservatory 10-4:30 daily, except Christmas and New Year's Day. $2 ($1 for children through high school) admission to conservatory, free to grounds. Conservatory and new gardens are accessible to wheelchair users.

NICHOLS ARBORETUM,
adjacent to the University of Michigan main campus; 1-313-998-7175, 7-3:30 daily. The park features 123 acres, a peony garden and native plants. Open 6 a.m.-10 p.m. daily. Free. Washington Heights entrance is accessible to wheelchair users.

Battle Creek

LEILA ARBORETUM,
West Michigan at 20th Street; 1-616-969-0270, 8:30-5 weekdays. Nearly 80-acre city park has ornamental trees and shrubs, an English landscape garden, perennials and conifers. Open dawn to dusk daily. Free. Not accessible to wheelchair users, but it is possible to drive through the grounds.

Bloomfield Hills

CRANBROOK HOUSE AND GARDENS,
380 Lone Pine Road; 1-810-645-3149, during hours of operation. Established in 1908, 40-acre garden includes extensive plantings, a reflecting pool and a wildflower garden. Open 10-5 Monday-Saturday, 11-5 Sunday from May through August. In September, open 1-5 Monday-Saturday, 11-5 Sunday. In October, hours are 12-4 weekends only. Admission $2, $1.50 for students and seniors. Partly accessible to wheelchair users.

Dearborn

HENRY FORD ESTATE,
on the campus of the University of Michigan-Dearborn; 1-313-593-5590, 8-5 weekdays. Landscaping by Jens Jensen highlights the grounds of this mansion. Open dawn to dusk daily. Free. Partly accessible to wheelchair users.

ARJAY MILLER MICHIGAN ARBORETUM
of Ford Motor Co., Michigan (U.S.-12) at Southfield (M-39); 1-313-322-0784, 9-4 daily. More than 1,000 Michigan trees and shrubs on 14 acres adjacent to Ford World Headquarters. Open dawn to dusk daily. Free. Accessible to wheelchair users.

Detroit

MOROSS HOUSE,
1460 E. Jefferson, 1-313-259-6363, during hours of operation. The 1840 garden was designed by the Garden Club of Michigan and is maintained by volunteers.

Features a gardening library. Open 9:30-3:30 Tuesday-Thursday. Free. Garden is accessible to wheelchair users.

ANNA SCRIPPS WHITCOMB CONSERVATORY,
Belle Isle; 1-313-267-7133 during hours of operation. The Victorian conservatory and formal gardens cover about 10 acres. Collections include the Palm House, orchids, ferns and a water lily garden. Open 10-5 daily. $1 admission includes entry to aquarium next door. Accessible to wheelchair users.

Dryden

SEVEN PONDS NATURE CENTER,
3854 Crawford Road, 1-810-796-3200, during hours of operation. This spot has 273 acres of natural habitats, herb, butterfly and spring wildflower gardens. Affiliated with Michigan Audubon Society. Open 9-5 Tuesday-Sunday except Thanksgiving, Christmas and New Year's Day. Admission $1.50, 75 cents for those 16 and younger. Partially accessible to wheelchair users.

East Lansing

MICHIGAN STATE UNIVERSITY HORTICULTURAL DEMONSTRATION GARDENS,
Bogue Street at Wilson Road, next to MSU's Plant and Soil Sciences Building; 1-517-355-0348, 9-5 weekdays. Site is 7.5 acres; includes a 4-H Children's Garden, perennial beds, All-America trial gardens, rose garden with All-America Rose Selection winners. Open dawn to dusk daily; teaching greenhouse open 8-5 weekdays. Free. Parking ($1 weekdays) for 80 cars adjacent. Accessible to wheelchair users.

W.J. BEAL BOTANICAL GARDEN,
adjacent to the library on West Circle Drive; 1-517-355-7750, 8-4 weekdays, for guided tours. Established in 1873, this is the oldest continuously operated outdoor botanical garden in the United States. About 5,000 species. Open dawn to dusk daily. Free. Walkways accessible to wheelchair users.

Grand Rapids

FREDERIK MEIJER GARDENS,
located on 70 acres at 3411 Bradford N.E.; 1-616-957-1580, 8-5 weekdays. Expected to open in spring of 1995. Among the features will be indoor and outdoor classrooms, a formal garden, nature trails, a sculpture collection, a library and a 15,000-square-foot conservatory.

Grosse Pointe Shores

EDSEL & ELEANOR FORD HOUSE,
1100 Lake Shore; 1-313-884-4222, during hours of operation. Most of the 63 acres are open to visitors. Landscaping and pool designed by Jens Jensen. Rose garden. Open noon-5 Wednesday-Sunday. Grounds only, $2. Mostly accessible to wheelchair users.

Kalamazoo

FIVE SENSES GARDEN,
John F. Kennedy School, 1411 Oakland Drive. One-half acre with three circular gardens to demonstrate sensory enrichment through plantings. Maintained by Gardenettes Garden Club. Open all the time. Free. Accessible to wheelchair users.

KALAMAZOO NATURE CENTER,
7000 N. Westnedge Ave.; 1-616-381-1574, during hours of operation. The 1,000-acre site includes a hummingbird and butterfly garden, as well as natural areas and plantings to attract birds. Open 9-5 Monday-Saturday, 1-5 Sunday, except Christmas Day. Nonmembers $3 adults, $1.50 children. Partly accessible to wheelchair users.

Lansing

COOLEY GARDENS,
Capitol and Main streets; 1-517-483-4282 anytime. Nearly a century old,

recently renovated by the City of Lansing, the 1.4-acre garden includes picnic sites. Open dawn to dusk. Free. Partly accessible to wheelchair users.

Marquette

MARQUETTE BRANCH PRISON,
1960 US-41 South; 1-906-226-6531, 9-5 daily. Recently renovated garden, water fountain and plantings. Drive through or walk. Open dawn to dusk daily. Free. Paths not accessible to wheelchair users.

Midland

DOW GARDENS,
Eastman Road at West St. Andrews; 1-517-631-2677, during hours of operation. 100-acre facility includes bulbs, annuals, perennials, wildflowers, 800 types of woody plants, a sensory trail, All-America Display Garden, test bedding plant area and a 4,000-square-foot greenhouse. Open 10-sunset daily except Thanksgiving, Christmas and New Year's Day; half-days Christmas Eve and New Year's Eve. $2 adults, children 5 and younger free. Accessible to wheelchair users.

CHIPPEWA NATURE CENTER,
400 S. Badour; 1-517-631-0830, during hours of operation. On 1,000 acres, the center includes a wildflower garden, an arboretum of native trees and shrubs, and an 1870 homestead with herb and heritage garden. Open 8-5 weekdays, 9-5 Saturday, 1-5 Sunday; trails open dawn to dusk daily. Closed Thanksgiving and Christmas; generally open 1-5 other holidays. Free, donations accepted. Paved trails are accessible to wheelchair users.

Niles

FERNWOOD BOTANIC GARDEN,
13988 Range Line Road; 1-616-695-6491 during hours of operation. More than 3,000 types of plants, an arboretum, prairie reconstruction and trails on 105 acres. Fern conservatory has 100 species. Open 10-6 Tuesday-Sunday, until dusk Friday, except Thanksgiving, Christmas and New Year's Day. $3 adults, $2 seniors, 12 and under free. Mostly accessible to wheelchair users.

Rochester Hills

MEADOW BROOK HALL
on the Oakland University campus; 1-810-370-3140, 8:30-4:30 daily. Approximately 10 acres of gardens, including about 20 permanent gardens surrounding the mansion, fountains and other water features, a natural wooded area, and a children's garden. Open dawn to dusk daily. Grounds admission free. Partially accessible to wheelchair users.

Royal Oak

DETROIT ZOOLOGICAL PARK,
Woodward Avenue at 10 Mile; 1-810-398-0900 anytime. Animals are the main draw here, but the landscaping on more than 125 acres is noteworthy and gets better every year. Many gardens are adopted and maintained by individuals or groups. Between May and October, hours are 10-5 daily, until 8 Wednesday from mid-June through August; November to April, 10-4 Wednesday-Sunday. Closed Thanksgiving, Christmas Day and New Year's Day. Admission $6 for adults, $4 for people over 62, and $3 for ages 2-12. Parking cars and vans $3. Accessible to wheelchair users.

Saginaw

LUCILLE E. ANDERSON MEMORIAL GARDEN,
120 Ezra Rust Drive; 1-517-759-1362, 8-5 weekdays. City park includes a perennial garden, a rose display and a central fountain with new Marshall Fredericks statue. Open 8-8 daily. Free. Accessible to wheelchair users.

JAPANESE CULTURAL CENTER AND TEA HOUSE,

527 Ezra Rust Drive; 1-517-759-1648, during hours of operation. Authentic Japanese tea house highlights the garden established with assistance from Saginaw's sister city in Japan. Stone lanterns, bridge, waterfall and stream make this a popular wedding site. Part of City of Saginaw parks system. Open 12-4 Tuesday-Saturday and 1-4 Sunday from Memorial Day through Labor Day. After Labor Day, it's closed on Sunday. From December through February the garden is closed except to groups. From March to Memorial Day, it's again open 12-4 Tuesday-Saturday. Closed on holidays year-round. Gardens free. Tours $3 for adults, for those under 12 or students $1.50; tea ceremony $6. Accessible to wheelchair users.

Tipton

HIDDEN LAKE GARDENS,
6280 W. Munger Road; 1-517-431-2060, during visitor center hours. Michigan State University owns and operates this 755-acre garden in the Irish Hills. It includes an All-America selection annual garden and a perennial garden, a primrose collection, a conservatory, a lake, a picnic area, six miles of paved drive, five miles of hiking trails, dwarf and rare conifers, and a hosta collection. From April through October, grounds are open 8 to dusk daily. From November through March, grounds open 8-4 daily. Visitor center is open 8-4:30 weekdays, 10-6 weekends and holidays. Admission during April-October is $1 weekdays, $3 weekends and holidays; during November-March, admission is $1 any day. Mostly accessible to wheelchair users.

Toledo, Ohio

TOLEDO BOTANICAL GARDEN,
5403 Elmer Drive; 1-419-536-8365, 8-4 weekdays. Sixty-five-acre site has a shade garden, gazebo, pond and aquatics collection, herb garden, perennial garden, daylily walk, cottage garden. Grounds are open 8 a.m.-9 p.m. daily, April through October. Free. Mostly accessible to wheelchair users.

White Cloud

LODA LAKE WILDFLOWER SANCTUARY,
inside Manistee National Forest; 1-616-689-6696, 9-4 weekdays. Native plants, one-mile trail around the lake with interpretive guide sheet. Small picnic area. Free. Not accessible to wheelchair users.

Windsor, Ontario

Call the city parks system at 1-519-255-6270, 8:30-4:30 weekdays, for more information. All are free and accessible to wheelchair users.

JACKSON PARK,
corner of Ouellette and Tecumseh. Sixty-four-acre site, built 1929, includes sunken gardens, fountains, formal gardens, 500 types of roses, including 12,500 individual plants established in 1967. Open daily dawn to midnight.

REAUME PARK AND COVENTRY GARDENS,
Riverside Drive at Pillette. These adjacent parks, established in 1935 and 1975, comprise 11.7 acres. The Peace Fountain, anchored offshore in the bay, highlights informal gardens, walkways and topiary. Open daily dawn to midnight.

DIEPPE PARK,
Riverside at Ouellette. Five acres, including roses and the Piazza Udine, three-tiered marble fountain. Open daily dawn to midnight.

OJIBWAY PRAIRIE COMPLEX,
5200 Matchette; 1-519-966-5852, during hours of operation. This 345-acre center includes more than 200 types of plants in a tall grass prairie, wetland and woods. Nature center. Open 10-5 daily except Dec. 25-26, New Year's Day, Good Friday.

PLANNING GRID

NOTES

PHONE NUMBERS

USDA PLANT HARDINESS ZONE MAP

The U.S. Department of Agriculture divides the country into hardiness zones based on winter low temperatures. This is the map section covering Michigan.

Plants are listed in catalogs and reference books as being hardy to a particular zone. For instance, Detroit and parts of southeastern Michigan are Zone 6, meaning anticipated winter lows of minus 10 to zero. Parts of the western Upper Peninsula are Zone 3, or minus 40 to minus 30.

Sometimes a plant is so temperature-tolerant that its zone rating doesn't matter much, as in the case of a plant listed as hardy in Zones 3-9. But especially when trying something new, check the USDA hardiness zones to make sure the plant has a chance of surviving in your area.

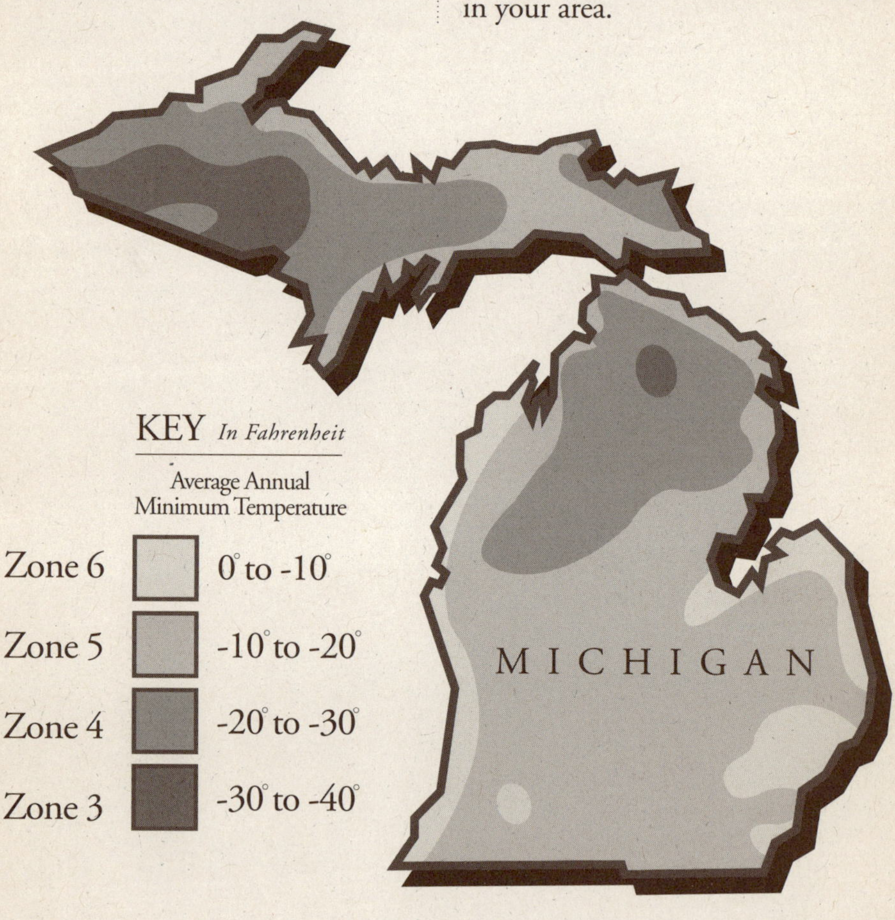